A Little Braver,

from Love, Delusion and, The Pain

Mehreen Syed

First published in 2020 by

Becomeshakespeare.com

One Point Six Technologies Pvt Ltd.
119-123, 1st Floor, Building J2, B - Wing,
WadalaTruck Terminal, Wadala East, Mumbai,
Maharashtra, India, 400022.
T:+91 8080226699

Wordit Art Fund helps deserving authors publish their work by providing monetary support. To apply for funding, please visit us at www.BecomeShakespeare.com

©

ISBN - 978-93-90463-07-7

Preface

This book comprises of short poetry. Few poems are being addressed to the one the writer was in love with; few poems are about how the writer had felt throughout this journey of love and heartbreak; and few are being addressed to the reader.

Dedicated to the dear reader

Don't be afraid to express your emotions,
Be afraid of expressing them to wrong people

Love can never make you weak,
If you feel so, this isn't love.

You have been punishing yourself for your mistakes all of
your life,
At least stop punishing yourself for someone else's mistakes.

Stop taking yourself for granted,
They have been doing so to you already

Let the fire burn inside of you,
Only then you can enlighten your world.

Thousands of us hide thousands of stories, with the fear of
being judged,
Why don't we just make this world as open as we pretend
it to be?

• Mehreen Syed

Contents

When you confessed your love

The day you came to me confessing your love,

I bared my soul naked to you, knowing that you may choose
to walk away.

I told you how broken I was and how little faith I had left
in love.

You came close to me, held my hand tightly,

whispered into my ear, that you accepted me the way I am.

You told me to believe you, so that you could prove,

that I was just scared of betrayals and not the love.

The softness of your voice and that gentleness in your
words, insisted me to trust.

Do you remember all of this, because I wish you did...

I still don't feel dare enough to cross that bridge,

the bridge where you said all this to me.

All these lines haunt me now, my love .

Do you still want to know why can't I let you go ?

• Cherry

You taught me love

I was broken by heart, refusing to let anyone come close to me,

you landed up and told me the world wasn't the way I believe.

I had gone through rough experiences, and expected love to be fake,

You landed up, told me I had to let it go and give myself a break.

Doesn't all this make you feel guilty even once, had you come to me to fix my heart once, so that you could break it more worse?

Or should I say,

You taught me love, so that I never ever wish to be in love again.

• *Cherry*

Was love there ?

"Love is right there; all you need is to believe me", you said.

Do I have to remind you of those old conversations,

where you told me love was there?

It's just those words, that made me hold on to you so long.

In spite of this pain that you gave me,

that has cursed within to set myself free.

I have been holding on to you so tightly,

because you have once told me love is right there.

But this time you weren't ready to believe,

When my love was actually there.

• *Cherry*

Mutual

If this bond was mutual to us, then why did I

have to fight for your attention?

If we both shared the same love, then why did I have to

ask for your time?

If this feeling of togetherness was what we both wanted,

then why did I have to beg you to let me see you once?

Something was wrong, or all of it was a lie.

It was never mutual, you had just been faking the love.

• *Cherry*

Priority

I am sorry that I made you my first priority, knowing

that, to you, I wasn't even just a priority.

I am sorry for crying those number of times, complaining

to you to make me a priority.

I am sorry I was so innocently foolish to understand,

That priority can never be asked, it has to be gifted.

I am sorry that I had gifted you this whole-heartedly,

knowing that you never appreciated this gift.

Yes, I am sorry that I made you my first priority.

• *Cherry*

Poisonous words

Your words were more dangerous than poison to my soul.

You killed every expectation of mine with those words of yours.

You spoke so harsh to me, not realising it ever how badly your words had been impacting me.

I was in love with you, everything you said meant value to me.

But how would you understand that? You don't know what it means to be in love.

You were never in love with me, so everything I said never meant any value to you.

• Cherry

Did you not know

When I was asked about you, I said he is an angel to me.

Did you not know, angels don't change?

When I was questioned about you, I said, I was in safe hands.

Did you not know, safe hands don't cause destruction?

When I was doubted about you , I said he is peace to my chaos.

Did you not know, peace doesn't bring storms to life?

Did you not know all of this ?

• Cherry

Why didn't you

I kept telling you that nobody was ever going to be in power, to separate us; because my love for you was deep enough.

Why didn't you tell me, that I should have opted out your name from it ?

I kept telling you I was ready to fight for you with my destiny, why didn't you tell me, I would end up fighting with you, for not getting your love ?

WHY DIDN'T YOU ?

• Cherry

I wasn't understanding

You said I wasn't understanding enough.

I couldn't understand it, when you took me for granted.

I couldn't understand it, when you didn't show up for months.

I couldn't understand it, when you refused to hear my cries.

I couldn't understand it, when I felt unattended by you.

Where was I supposed to be understanding, I couldn't understand that actually.

• *Cherry*

False convincing

I started convincing myself, that's how it is supposed to work, and forced myself to settle for what I was getting.

But my body and soul responded differently, my self-esteem screamed back and I developed a hatred for self, full of anxiety and lack of life was the sign.

This is where I realized I was false convincing my own self.

• Cherry

Your actions

The note I wrote down to you, mentioned you to be favourite memory of my college life.

The actions you had for me made my life haunted for ever.

The love I had for you, saw you as a king of my kingdom.

The actions that you had for me, made me feel like I was a slave there.

The little girl inside of me, was seeing you as her saviour from the rest of the world.

The actions that you had for me, made me look for safe shelter away from you.

So tell me, are you still going to say you didn't betray me? Just tell me...

So tell me didn't your actions murder my emotions?

• *Cherry*

I stayed long enough

I tried enough to make it sure, that I don't regret if I left.

So I don't regret leaving, because there was nothing

I could do anymore, to make you feel the way I did.

So when I stand here right now,

I believe this I am not regretting walking away.

What I regret is staying long enough,

to let you destroy me completely.

• Cherry

I was losing myself

Everytime I cried in front of you ,

I was being told, I was reason for my own tears.

The rage in me wanted to tell you loudly.

It's you who is wrong, whose way is wrong,

stop making me feel otherwise.

But I chose to stay silent, suppressing my inner voice,

because I thought I would loose you,

but forgot that I am losing myself.

• Cherry

I gave my best

I cared for you, while knowing that you don't care about me.

I put you as my first choice, knowing that I am an option to you.

I loved you so deeply, knowing that you believed our bond to be temporary yet.

I believed you to be my world, knowing that you don't consider me as a family

I gave my best, knowing that you were not trying even least.

I gave my best, with the hope that you were going to realise it one day.

• Cherry

I chose you

The world knew me as a girl, who was confident, and I chose you to see my insecurities.

The world saw me as a person, who was tough to break, and I chose you to see my scars.

The world saw me as someone who was bold to speak for self, and I chose you to see my fears.

But you chose to make me regret for choosing you over everything.

• Cherry

You called me lovesick

I tried acting like you did ,but I failed.

I tried not feeling excited for meeting you, the way you never had been, but I failed.

I tried not wanting to talk to any more, the way you didn't, but I failed.

I tried acting cold while claiming to be in love, the way you had been, but I failed.

Why didn't you tell me that you weren't in love, rather than telling me that I was lovesick?

I asked for care from the one who I was in love with.

I asked the attention of the one who claimed to love me.

I asked for the love that you had showed me once.

If asking for what I deserve was being lovesick,

then darling, I am going to be lovesick for all my life,

because this is how love is supposed to me,

for not having enough of someone you love.

• Cherry

If you had told me

I would have respected it, if you had chosed to tell me, that you were out of love, even though you had promised not to.

I would have accepted you to be like everyone else, though you had promised you were different.

But what I couldn't accept was:

That you chose to blame me, for falling out of love, knowing that I was the only one, trying so hard to make you stay there.

You chose to end up by, making me feel miserable about being in love,

so that you could escape easily while I will end up blaming myself for it.

• *Cherry*

Million chances

For those million chances that I gave you, for which you misunderstood me as weak enough to not be able to walk away.

For those million explanations that I gave you, for which you misunderstood me as crazy enough, not to be able to accept the truth.

You need to know, I was not weak; I was never crazy.

I just was stronger enough to hold on to you, in spite of those harsh conditions you had put me in.

YES, you needed to know that, I was never weak.

• *Cherry*

Emotions

I started seeing my emotions as a problem, because you told me I was over-emotional.

I started seeing my tears as weakness, every time they came out when you got me mistreated.

I started ignoring my emotional needs, because all you made me understand was, to be practical.

I started changing myself and forcing my heart not to feel, because you told me I was not acting mature in love.

I started hating myself slowly and you loved it, didn't you ?

• *Cherry*

Official

Which love on this earth needs official validation, to be selfless?

Which love in a heart needs documentation, to be concerning?

Which love in a soul needs recognition, to be protective?

Then what kind of love made you to tell me,

That ours wasn't official yet for you to be concerned for me?

• *Cherry*

Coward

You were a coward,

for awakening love in a person without the intention of keeping it alive for ever.

You were a coward for making someone fall for you, without the intention of catching her.

You were a coward, for breaking a person, who believed you, when everything was standing against you.

Yes, you were a coward, for winning my heart and then making me feel like I was just a trophy, to be kept in some corner of your home.

You were a coward,

For betraying someone in love, who already feared it.

You made that human more lifeless.

You were a big coward.

• *Cherry*

Proved me wrong instead

I wanted our love story to be an example.

I wanted to prove people wrong, who said we can't make it together.

I wanted it to be a beautiful tale, that stays alive for ever.

But look, you chose to prove me wrong instead.

• Cherry

I was never even a part of your world

"Please don't leave me, it's been two years already.

I can't let you go.

It is a lifetime that I have imagined with you.

I won't be able to live anymore" I said this to you.

"People leave after 10 years, these were just two", you replied.

This line took the life out of me.

I was imagining my life with you, you didn't even think of me while imagining yours.

You were the one I considered my world.

I wasn't even a part of yours.

• Cherry

Comfort in pain

I saw myself getting comfortable in that pain.

I refused growth and denied my soul that things were given wrong to it.

I wanted to move away , but I was so used to this pain that I didn't dare to look out.

I was ready to compromise and die suffocating, because I was getting comfortable with that pain.

I forgot the world outside was too beautiful, to live this way, because I was getting used to that pain.

• Cherry

I don't feel ashamed

To deny that you walked away,

I am not going to pretend that I didn't care.

I would still love to accept that I was the only one who loved,

and I was the only who wanted to stay.. because I feel no shame
in that.

I would rather feel ashamed if I pretend I didn't care either,
and didn't wanted you to stay.

Because my pride isn't what I live for, but my love for you
was what I ought to live for.

I don't feel ashamed to admit that I begged you to stay,

because my love for you didn't allow me to let you go.

The only thing I rather felt ashamed of,

Is that my self love was so low,

that I had to ask love from you.

• *Cherry*

I haven't felt the rain since then

I haven't felt the rain since then.

You told me to wait for you always,

And not to get wet in the rain alone ever.

It's been a year that I am waiting for you to remember it.

Whenever it rains, it's a promise, that I remember.

Everyone around is telling me, the weather is beautiful.

But I haven't felt it since then.

Please set me free from that promise,

Because even this rain is a reminder of my pain.

• Cherry

Ask your soul if it is still alive

It's now that I need healing, because you broke me,

but darling, you needed healing since always.

Ask yourself, if your soul is alive, because I knocked your door a number of times, and no one heard me there.

Darling, its you who needs healing because you can't respond to emotions.

It's not my soul that needs healing, because it feels.

my love, it was your soul that needed healing, because you have forgotten to feel.

Do yourself a favour; listen to what your soul has to say,

It wants to feel; coldness is not what it needs.

You haven't been sincere to your soul; how I wished you were sincere to me.

• *Cherry*

Life is never about chasing

You told me you wanted me; you got me and so you love me.

But then I was made to chase you.

And you in turn, chased your new selfish motives.

To you, life was chasing a thing after thing.

But I pray you don't spend life chasing, and

don't make people to chase either.

Because life is no good this way,

I felt misery while chasing you.

Stop chasing and stop making people chase,

It's just draining life from you and from the ones who love you.

• *Cherry*

Help

You were never expressive and I felt you needed my help.

I did everything to be your friend, before I could be your partner.

I asked you to share your problems with me and trust me as a best friend.

All you did was drain me back out of my emotions and made me feel psychic.

I didn't know, you had chosen to be this way, because you felt being expressive in a relationship was stupid.

While trying to be there for your help, I ended up crying for my own help.

• Cherry

Old person in you

I couldn't hold on so long, because that old person in you,

that I was in love with, had just not left me;

It had left you too.

Thus, I couldn't hold on so long.

• *Cherry*

Don't tell me I have to wait

Don't tell me I have to wait ,

So that we can make it together.

If I don't belong to your present, then Mister,

I don't want your future.

• Cherry

Scariest moment

You want to know how did it feel, when you chose to walk away.

It was the scariest moment ever, when you told this to my face.

It felt as if you had put your hand inside my chest,

Squeezed my heart hardly and badly as possible.

I screamed helplessly in front of you, begging you, saying it was hurting worse.

I begged you asking to stop once,

Because my heart was aching out of pain.

When I looked into your eyes, they had the scariest message to tell.

They told me clearly that they never felt anything for me.

That look in your eyes, I am never going to forget.

That cold look you had for me, I am never going to forget.

• *Cherry*

Unwillingness

Your unwillingness for everything was a sign,

that I shouldn't have ignored.

• Cherry

Narcissist

You were a narcissist, and I refused to accept that.

You drained me emotionally, and I kept looking for excuses.

You drained me off my life, and made me suffer,

and I kept believing your lies.

You used to make me feel sorry, for not just my mistakes, but yours as well.

• *Cherry*

Why?

If this coldness was your way of life,

you should have showed it back then, when you approached
me.

If this darkness was your home,

why did you show me a home full of light?

If you were a person with no life, then why did you put a ray
of hope in my life?

I want my answers; I want to ask you why???

Why did you fool me all the time???

• Cherry

Take this pain away

My nights are sleepless, and

my mornings are hopeless.

I wished for you to come; if not for a stay,

but at least to take this pain away.

• Cherry

If this love wouldn't have been there

When I was crying in front of you, asking you not to leave me, telling you that nobody could love you the way I do.

All you said was "there are thousands like me out there on the roads".

I wished the earth to engulf me; the sky to cover me up.

The breath stopped inside of me, but I was still alive, This life felt like a burden now.

I hated myself.

I hated the love for you inside of me.

If this love wouldn't have been there, I wouldn't have let you laugh at my condition.

If this love for you wouldn't have been there?

I wouldn't have let you have warmth from the fire I was burning in.

I wouldn't have let you murder my self-esteem.

If this love for you wouldn't have been there, the story would have been different.

Though it was not love that hurt me, it was indeed love for a wrong person like you.

• Cherry

If you had loved me back

I showered you with all the love in universe, even though I was just getting pain from you.

Imagine the scenario that could have been there, if you had just loved me back the way I did.

I would have built kingdoms for you.

I would have walked oceans for you.

I would have dived from the sky for you.

I would have lived for you, and I would died happily for you, and what not.

Just imagine if you had chosen to love me instead.

• Cherry

That's all I wanted

I never asked for a bouquet of roses,

One rose would have been enough.

Candle-light dinners weren't what I wanted,

Street food would have been enough.

I never asked for holidays,

one sunset was what I craved for.

I never asked you to pamper me all the time,

but a little love in my bad time could have done

wonders to my life.

I never asked all of you,

a little of you would have been enough.

• Cherry

When you were drifting away slowly

When you were slowly drifting away,

the music around stopped being melodic to me,

the beauty of weather around felt irritating to me,

the child in me stopped liking to play,

the happiness felt little low, the sorrows felt a little more,

the future started seeming scary,

the life felt not happening anymore,

the fairy tales started losing meaning to me.

All this started happening when you were drifting away slowly .

• Cherry

I feared your loss

I asked them, how would I know if I was in love,

They said I will fear their loss; only then maybe.

But they fear me now,

when I feared their loss.

Maybe it was too deep with me;

That they couldn't believe.

• Cherry

Our story

I can't even call our story a love story, because you are too disgraced to be called a lover.

• *Cherry*

It's been a decade

It's been a decade, but I haven't been able to forget,

all those places where you came to meet me.

• Cherry

I wasn't supposed to stay

To the one who said he won't leave, you left.

If I have to put it in a better way, you pushed me away.

After all which person is supposed to stay there, while they are being disrespected and mistreated.

After all which person is supposed to stay there, while they are made to feel unattended and unwanted.

After all which person is supposed to stay there,

while they are made to feel desperate for being deeply in love.

I wasn't supposed to stay

• Cherry

I feel shame for you

I feel shame for you as a person,

for telling me that you didn't touch me ever,

so I had no right to ask for any kind of justice.

I feel shame for you as a person,

for telling me,

you could have done anything to my body,

because I was madly in love with you,

but it was your goodness that you chose not to.

I feel shame for your thinking, Mister, that made you tell me this.

I hadn't made you an owner of my body,

I had made you the saviour of my heart.

I feel shame for the way you have uprooted yourself.

• *Cherry*

Decision

Do you know how many nights I spent fighting back myself,
To not to take a decision of walking away?

Do you know how much it took for me to suppress my gut feeling,

To accept that you didn't love me ever?

Do you know how many times I killed my logic,

To accept that you had been taking me for granted?

Do you know how much it cost me mentally,

To murder my self respect while you continued mistreating me.

I wish you knew how much it made me suffer to stay there, while it was hurting.

You didn't know anything, you just knew nothing

Else you wouldn't have continued to make me bleed.

• *Cherry*

Walking away

It didn't just take me one moment to walk away.

It didn't take me one decision to walk away.

It didn't just take me a time of one day or one night to walk away.

It was not just one tear that I wiped ,while walking away.

It was lot more:

It took me all of my life, that I had till now, to walk away.

It took me all of my emotions, to walk away.

It took me all of my strength to walk away.

Because walking away was a must now, since your mistreatment was worse now.

• Cherry

End of us

I chose silence this time,

I chose to leave, without even telling you this time.

I chose myself.

My words had no power on you anymore; I let silence lead my way.

For, no matter how long I would have been there, you would have still made me regret at the end.

So I did right.

I chose to leave you on your own.

• *Cherry*

Little sympathy

You made me feel so bad about myself, that I started questioning my worth.

Why didn't you show me a little sympathy,

By telling me you didn't love me enough to see my worth?

I wish you had showed me a little sympathy,

By telling me you didn't value my love; I would have walked away very early.

Tell me why didn't you show me a little sympathy ?

• *Cherry*

Misunderstood love

All along I kept blaming love, for this hurt.

I blamed love for getting me this pain.

I misunderstood love for making me suffer.

I cursed love for not being right to me.

Lately;

I realised, it was never love that brought me suffering.

I realized it was never love, that troubled me.

It was indeed love with a wrong person, that I misunderstood love.

• *Cherry*

Unlove

How did you fell out of love, and

when did you fell out of love?

Because, irrespective of your abusive behaviour,

I have been struggling with unloving you.

I wanted to unlove you the way you did, but I

couldn't, in spite of your unkindness and you did,

in of my kindness.

Teach me how to unlove.

• Cherry

A stranger who was known once

I tried hating you, but couldn't.

I didn't know how to hate the one,

who once was my world,

who was once the love of my life,

who once was exactly what I wanted,

I can't punish myself to hate you .

But that doesn't mean I love you still.

It's just that I let you go back, to the world of strangers.

Those strangers whose opinion doesn't matter to my worth.

But you are a stranger with memories, a stranger who was known once.

I can't undo that.

• Cherry

Someday you will

Someday you will crave for the love like I did,

If not from me, but maybe from someone else.

Someday you will long to see someone like I did,

If not me, but maybe someone else.

Someday your emotions will be ignored,

If not by me, but maybe by someone else.

Someday you will feel haunted by the fake promises,

like I have been.

Someday you will be in love, but you won't be loved.

Someday surely.

• *Cherry*

Where are you now?

You wished me to accept you in front of this world; the same world asks, where are you now?

• *Cherry*

Does it bother you ?

Does it bother you that someone doesn't believe in love anymore because of you?

Or does it bother that someone's definition of forever has changed because of you?

While being that someone who has lost all this,

I would never wish to be the one because of whom someone loses all this.

I am relieved in this pain then, if being there gives you any joy.

I would never wish to be someone, because of whom someone loses faith in love .

I will rather wish to be the one who lost it, because of someone like you.

• *Cherry*

Maybe I will forgive you someday

I went to the Gurudwara to seek my answers

I cried near a mandir, to get a cure for my pain

I screamed outside a masjid, to look for a way

I put my heart out, inside a church.

I knocked at every door where they said, God resides.

To wherever the God resides, I asked him to give justice to me.

Maybe I will forgive you someday, but God won't, because you gave such a misery to its creature that God witnessed.

God helps those who help themselves; rightly said.

• *Cherry*

You can't heal me

I have hated the thought that,

you were the only one who could heal me.

I didn't know why I hated this thought, until I realized,

"The ones who break you, can't heal you"

Yes it's what I knew always, but it took me time to accept.

You can never be the one who could heal me back.

Since you were the one who broke me.

It was indeed "me" who could fix me.

• Cherry

Karma

Do you remember you told me once,

that karma takes over on everyone?

I want to believe you for this.

Pray that it comes to be true.

Because I wish to see you right once.

I wish karma to take over on us.

All I have witnessed is your lies.

I wish, this time I witness a truth from you.

I wish karma to take over on you.

• *Cherry*

You never deserved

I have lost precious moments to you,

thinking that you were the one.

I had reserved myself for someone who deserves me and those precious moments.

But I lost myself to someone, who never deserved me.

• *Cherry*

Escaping me

Can I escape these days and nights, that remind me of you?

Help me to escape everything that ends on you.

I can't hold on to this life for long; I am scared.

Can you help me to have a grip on it? I am trying to escape everything.

I am escaping me.

I don't deserve this.

Every step I walk; word I talk,

Everything such thing that is in me,

Everything that makes me;

Its suffering. Help me..

• *Cherry*

I cried

Under a naked sky, laying down on my knees,

I cried, cried and cried.

The sky was crying with me.

It was raining heavily.

The rain was washing away my tears.

The tears were washing away my pain.

I cried, until my eyes were weary.

But the pain was still heavy.

• Cherry

I don't want to come back to you, like I did always

I don't want to come back, like I did always, just to realise it again and again, that I don't mean anything to you.

I don't want to come back to you , like I did always, just to see, that I can never see the person in you that I once thought you were.

I don't want to come back to you, like I did always, just to see that it is me who only loved truly and you just faked it.

I don't want to come back, as I did always, because this time I won't be able to pick myself up back again.

I don't want to come back to you this time, like I used to, even if this loneliness and pain make me bleed to death.

Because at least, I will die witnessing a bravery in me; a bravery of not letting this soul get anymore mistreated.

• *Cherry*

You were not the only one to cause me pain

I didn't feel good the way you had been treating me, the way you didn't value me.

I wanted to hate you for that, but then I realized I was doing no good to myself either.

You were not the only one to cause pain to me, I was also a part of it,

because how could I be so cruel to my soul who was crying out of pain, by staying right there, seeing you mistreating me !

• Cherry

The only thing we had in common

We had a thing in common.

All I cared about, was you.

And all you cared about, was just you.

Yes we had a thing in common.

• *Cherry*

I did right

I kept telling you that nobody was ever going to be in power, to separate us .Because my love for you was deep enough.

Why didn't you told me ,that I should have opted out your name from it ?

I kept telling you I was ready to fight for you with my destiny, why didn't you told me, I would end up fighting you, for not Getting your love ?

WHY DIDN'T YOU ?

• Cherry

How am I supposed to

I am not just struggling with this pain only,

I am struggling with forgiving you also.

Because they say, it's a must that I forgive you,

to make peace with myself.

But how am I supposed to not hold grudges for someone, who shattered my dreams?

How am I supposed to forgive the one, who made me feel like a corpse?

How am I supposed to forgive the one, who responded my love with an abusive behaviour?

How am I supposed to?

I am struggling with forgiving you.

I am struggling to make peace with myself.

• Cherry

If someday I forget

If someday I forget how did I feel about you once; I am writing this to not forget, that how did you made me feel.

If someday I forget how much you meant to me once;

I am writing this to not to forget,

that I meant nothing more than a time pass to you.

If someday my heart craves you again out of loneliness,

I am writing this to make it remember why it had to leave.

If someday I forget to make sure if the new person is right for me,

I am writing this to not to forget, if his actions resembled yours.

• *Cherry*

To make me realise

Coming close to you was necessary, to make myself realise, why didn't we have a way together.

Giving you all those chances was a must, to make myself realise, what was making it fail all the time.

Trying to make you convince was important, to make myself realise, I later don't regret giving it up.

Asking you for your time and attention was right, to make me realise, my pride doesn't let our attachment die.

• Cherry

War with self

It was now a fight with my own self.

Facing the world with these open scars was the ugliest phase.

Waking up in the morning and laying back in the night was the difficult part.

Living the reality that I never wanted to happen, was the scariest thing.

After cry, I ended up seeing myself hanging there.

Everything just reminded me of how unwanted and unworthy I had felt.

• Cherry

I kept telling myself

Not knowing if it was going to be okay ever,

the way I was feeling,

But I kept telling to the inner me

Please, don't give up. This is preparing you for the best.

Please, don't give up; things are going to be ok.

I know you're tired, but please don't give up; peace isn't that far.

Please don't give up; you are a warrior."

• Cherry

The injustice

Someday you will be happily married, financially sound and satisfied about life.

The time, when you won't be chasing your selfish motives anymore; would you remember the tears I cried for you?

When the life will run in your veins,

Would you remember the love I craved for,

Or, are you going to be lifeless always?

When you would be doing justice to someone's love in your life,

Would you remember the injustice you did to me and my love?

• *Cherry*

Already broken

So does it make you a man of value any way,

Does it make you feel like a king,

Does it fuel your pride,

Or does it make you feel that you won in the battlefield,

By breaking someone who was already broken enough?

If that gives you satisfaction, then have it,

Congratulations! You broke someone who was already broken.

• *Cherry*

I am mourning my loss

I am not mourning your loss.

My heart isn't crying because I lost you.

These tears that aren't ready to stop, aren't for you.

Fellow, come here and I will tell you, how life has been to me.

Indeed I had a much big loss..

Fellow, show me some courtesy, I am mourning myself.

I have pity for me.

While I was looking for you,

I have lost this soul to darkness indeed.

• Cherry

Dear self

Dear self, I owe you a deep apology.

Whenever I get reminded,

of how you had been treated,

I feel guilty for not thinking about you once.

I feel sorry for my selfishness,

for being so much in love with someone else,

that I forgot to love you.

Dear self, I owe you a deep apology.

• Cherry

I am scared of my own self

I used to be scared of losing you; but now that I have lost you,

I am scared of myself, because this self isn't scared of anything else anymore.

• Cherry

Don't forget

Love as much as you want to.

Love as selflessly as you want to.

Love as hard as you can.

Love as honestly as you can.

Love as deep as you can.

But don't forget when to stop,

For the sake of self love.

• Cherry

Lost

You are not truly lost, if you still carry hope in your heart.

You are not truly lost, if you carry these scars as honorary badges.

You will find a way, if you still have kindness in your soul.

You will find a way, if you don't let hatredness overpower you.

If you did give up, only then you are truly lost.

So darling, don't you dare give up;

the universe has witnessed wonders, and so would you.

Keep going on.

• Cherry

I held faith in kindness

You tried every way to turn me lifeless,

I held on hard to kindness.

I held faith on this, that love doesn't bring misery.

I thank myself for this; for not turning cold like you have.

I thank myself for still believing, that compassion and hope is there yet.

I wouldn't want to live like the way you do.

I wouldn't want to be a moving corpse.

I am good this way, I am good that I feel.

• Cherry

Thank you

I won't thank you for this pain ,

But I will thank you for this experience.

I won't thank you for making me feel unworthy,

But I will thank you, that because of this,

I could realise my self worth.

I won't thank you for not responding to my love,

But I will thank you that because of this ,

I had to realise the importance of self love.

I won't thank you for this pain ,

But yes, I thank you for these gains.

• Cherry

Dear best friend

Dear best friend, I am sorry that I didn't listen to you ,

When you warned me about the red flags that you saw, before I could.

But dear best friend, please believe me, when I say that, it was something that wasn't in my hands.

I was in love blindly and wasn't ready to accept the devil in him.

But dear best friend, thank you for being there, even when I didn't listen to you.

• *Cherry*

Ask them

Before you heal someone, ask them,

if they are willing to give up the things,

that made them sick.

Else you will end up needing help for self-healing.

• Cherry

You give them attention

You start giving them attention,

and get them used to it,

then wonder why they are fighting for it,

when you start giving it to someone else.

• Cherry

Their love is limited

They are jumping from person to person,

telling each of them, they are in love.

How ashamed it is to see, that their love is

just limited to the outer beauty of the body,

that fades away within no time.

How ashamed it is to witness,

that their love changes from body to body.

• *Cherry*

It's not working anymore

You start chasing new selfish motives,

and put least efforts in what's already there.

And then you end up saying,

it's not working anymore.

• *Cherry*

Your Trueness

I am not fond of kids; I am fond of innocence they have.

Kid would never wish pain back on anyone,

because, they have no selfish desires.

I tried to be fond of all mankind, but they gave me nothing;
just pain.

This rudeness, unkindness, dishonesty won't make anyone
fond of you.

Your trueness would.

• *Cherry*

You ain't wrong

You ain't the one who has misunderstood,

you were actually looking for what you deserved.

Their false masks killed the hope inside of you.

Whatever you know, isn't false,

Whatever you have been forced to settle for, is false indeed.

You knew the right thing ,you had the true hope.

Believe yourself for this.

• Cherry

They have been deceiving us

They've been deceiving me and so did they to you,

They told they had everything I needed.

But they didn't know that I was the one to seek depths.

They tried to stop me by misleading.

This shallowness isn't what I am born for.

And this shallowness isn't what I am going to live for.

• Cherry

We run hiding our emotions

We run a lifetime hiding the emotions inside of us,

because we fear we will be judged.

The ones who show it to the world out there,

regret doing so, because people misunderstand it as their weakness.

Why can't we make the world as open as it pretends to be?

Why can't we understand the ones, who get their emotions out?

• *Cherry*

Be free from desires

You will be losing a lifetime,

Just to realise what you were seeking is in you.

The saints did find it; just not by mere solitude,

they just felt nothing was more worthy than this peace.

They didn't love the wandering,

They loved being the person that was free from desires.

• *Cherry*

Beautiful face

I don't want anyone to fall for my beauty,

because this beautiful face has never attracted a loyal heart.

I wish someday someone falls for the beauty of my soul and heart.

Only then I will get the justice for the love inside of me.

I felt no good with this beautiful face, because whoever it attracted was a curse to my soul.

• Cherry

My foolishness

My foolishness lead me to wander in mountains.

I went to charming faces and stores.

But they had no soul.

Just in search of peace.

I have been everywhere, wherever you have been thinking
to look for it.

Fellow, we have the same destination.

But you got to believe that no one offered it to me.

When every door closed on my face, when darkness was
deeper, when the sun in others refused to shine on me, when
their rains didn't soak my dryness.

I regretted my foolishness.

Peace is in me.

Peace is in you.

Don't wander fellow, just get beneath your soul.

Everything is right there.

• Cherry

Let these words help someone

I had no confidence to pen it down,

The pain inside me pushed me to.

I had no confidence to share it with the world outside,

But I didn't want anybody else to suffer the way I did, by a human like you.

Let it be how people respond to it,

I no longer care what others think of me.

Because it was just me who has gone through this journey,

It is just me who has walked this way alone.

Let these words help someone who is walking alone like I did.

Let someone else's thoughts not supress my voice anymore.

• Cherry

You have to love the Change

Fear of end,

Or the desire of more,

If anything you have,

you have to love the change.

I feared both.

• *Cherry*

Our generation

Why has our generation lost the meaning of love?

Why does our generation end up blaming love,

for something that they are actually responsible for?

Why is our generation misusing this beautiful feeling,

for their selfish motives?

How do you even call it love, if you are yet to understand
the depth of it?

How do you even call it love for ever, when your eyes are
still roaming around?

Why do you make someone lose faith in love, just because
you hadn't your faith in it yet?

True love among us is breathing its last.

Love is beautiful, love makes life worth to live.

Love is what this world seeks at the end of everything.

Our generation has lot to learn yet.

• *Cherry*

Love is a commitment

If you are really in love, you will never

lose interest,

Because being in love is a

commitment, and not an interest;

That has to be there even if you are not in a mood to be.

• *Cherry*

Find yourself someone

Find yourself someone, who doesn't see your vulnerability as a problem; rather helps you to make it your strength.

Find yourself someone, who doesn't tell you that you are overemotional; rather understands your emotions and helps you to overcome where ever needed.

Find yourself someone, who feels blessed to see the eagerness in you for meeting and seeing him.

Find yourself someone, who doesn't tell you that you are desperate for wanting to hear him more; rather, feels happy to see himself so valued and in turn, values you more.

Find yourself someone, whose actions make you feel that you are being loved and not just his words.

Find yourself a man who is looking to plan for a family with you; not a boy who is just chasing his selfish motives.

• Cherry

The heart knows its own rules

Attention isn't what my heart craved for,

But your attention is what it died for.

Not on hearing everyone's name, raised the beats of this heart;

Even this heart follows own rules.

I couldn't make this heart beat for someone else,

the way it knew to beat for you.

This heart follows its own rules.

This heart knows its own rules.

• *Cherry*

The heart is itself the pain

You could seek cure for the pain,

but what to look for,

if the heart itself becomes the pain?

• Cherry

Dear reader,

This pain broke me and made me.

It burnt me to the ashes and raised me to the heights of sky.

But you have to know,

Self love is cure to every pain.

And self belief has to be there, when even love lies.

• *Mehreen Syed*

Acknowledgments

Thank you

To the reader for giving a space in their heart, to this emotional journey .

To my loved ones for inspiring me to write my heart out.

And special thanks to the Wordit Art fund for making this project possible.